Mythical Beas...

GIANTS
AND
TROLLS

By Alice Peebles

Illustrated by Nigel Chilvers

HUNGRY
TOMATO™

"One eye stared madly, his hair stood on end, and his mouth stretched wide open in a terrible gape, showing sharp, dog-like teeth flecked with fiery sparks."

Contents

Giants and Trolls 6

Wolf-headed Humanoid: *Cynocephalus* 8

Three-in-one Warrior: *Geryon* 10

Fiend of the Forest: *Forest Troll* 12

All-seeing Herdsman: *Argus* 14

One-eyed Colossus: *Polyphemus* 16

Mountain Savage: *Mountain Troll* 18

Celtic Hero: *Cuchulain* 20

Cannibal Giants: *Laestrygonians* 22

Giant of Ice and Stone: *Hrungnir* 24

King of all Trolls: *King Troll* 26

Rogues' Gallery 28

Want to Know More? 30

Index 32

Giants and Trolls

Meet the top 10 biggest, meanest and most bloodthirsty creatures that stomped the world in ancient times...

Have you ever heard of Polyphemus, the fearsome Cyclops who had his one eye burnt out by the Greek hero, Odysseus? What about twelve-limbed Geryon, who fought to the death with Hercules? Or Cuchulain, a warrior of Irish folklore, who could actually grow in stature, spat out flecks of fire, and killed hundreds of men at a time?

Then there are the trolls, feared throughout Scandinavia for their massive size, ugly looks and fondness for tasty humans. Up those bleak and windswept mountaintops of northern Europe, very near the realm of the Norse gods, you'll also find Hrungnir, the stone-headed giant who quarrelled and fought with Thor himself. But which is the most ferocious of all? You're about to find out.

These 10 beasts are shown in vivid scenes that are based on a special moment in their stories — usually when they are about to crush a much, much smaller victim. They appear in ranked order of power from 10 to 1, with scores out of 10 for each of five categories: Strength, Repulsiveness, Special Powers, Ferocity and Invincibility. You'll also find a suggestion on how to defeat or neutralize each one — you, of course, are a lot more fortunate than any victim and can take time to work this out...

The details about each monster are inspired by mythology and folklore handed down since ancient times. Keep on reading to find out more about just how nasty these giants can be — they are, after all, the nastiest of the nasty that were around at the time! So, are you ready to join Odysseus and his men as they face the fury of cannibal giants, or share the fate of a wretched captive at the gloomy court of King Troll?

Wolf-headed Humanoid
Cynocephalus

Teeth bared in a wolfish grin, Cynocephalus leaned over his catch as it roasted on the fire. He could not wait for the tasty pig to be cooked. He tore off a leg and was about to sink his long pointed fangs into the pink meat when …

…snarling, another of his kind bounded out of the trees and snatched the bone from his hand. The thief backed away, growling, slobbering and chewing at the same time. Outraged, Cynocephalus leapt on his foe, howling and snapping at the flesh below the wolf's head. Soon they were a writhing, snarling, blood-streaked mass on the ground, fighting for supremacy – and meat.

How to defeat Cynocephalus

It is vital that Cynocephalus is unaware of any danger, so his acute senses of sight and smell must not be alerted. The answer might be to prepare an animal trap and, with a favourite prey as a lure, make sure that he falls right in.

Where does this myth come from?

A race of fierce, dog-headed, human-like creatures was first recorded in 400 BCE by a Greek physician. The great explorer Marco Polo also wrote about similar humanoids in the 13th century when he visited the island of Angamanain, now called the Andaman Islands, in the Bay of Bengal.

Beast Power

Strength	5
Repulsiveness	1
Special Powers	2
Ferocity	6
Invincibility	6

Total
20/50

Three-in-one Warrior
Geryon

Stealthily, Hercules began driving the red cattle of Geryon down to the shore of their island home. He not only had to steal them, but bring them back to his master, King Eurystheus. But a strange and mighty figure leapt in his path. It was the twelve-limbed, three-headed warrior, Geryon! Hercules could just see one of his three faces, twisted with fury.

His six arms flailing, Geryon rained down blows with sword and spear, desperate to draw the hero's blood. Hercules leapt and dodged and parried with his shield. Slowly he manoeuvred around so the dazzling sun fell into Geryon's eyes. In this brief moment, Hercules reached back and hurled his spear...

How to defeat Geryon

Like Hercules, an opponent would have to think of a clever trick to gain an advantage, perhaps by being so quick that Geryon might trip over and be mortally wounded by his own weapons.

Where does this myth come from?

In Greek mythology, Geryon features in the 10th labour of Hercules, as related by Apollodorus of Athens and other writers. He was the son of Callirrhoe, a water nymph-goddess, and Chrysaor, who was himself the son of Medusa. This perhaps explains Geryon's monstrous looks combined with immense strength.

Beast Power

Strength
6

Repulsiveness
2

Special Powers
1

Ferocity
7

Invincibility
6

Total
22/50

Fiend of the Forest
Forest Troll

One dank night a traveller plodded wearily through a forest far from home. Holding up his lantern, he saw a stone bridge ahead – and something else. A giant tree seemed to be moving towards him. But no – it was a beast with branches growing from its head and shoulders. Its face grimaced, showing a single tooth. A forest troll! Its eyes glowed red in the lantern light as it lifted a stone mallet, ready to take aim. The traveller, too terrified to cry out, turned and fled, desperate to get away, anywhere....

How to defeat a Forest Troll

Since trolls cannot take sunlight, they should be lured from their lair in daytime, perhaps by offering money to cross their bridge or land, and they will turn to stone.

8

Beast Power

Strength
7

Repulsiveness
6

Special Powers
1

Ferocity
7

Invincibility
5

Total
26/50

Where does this myth come from?

In the ancient language of Old Norse, the word troll means 'fiend' or 'monster' and describes a kind of hostile, extremely ugly giant. Trolls occur in Icelandic legends and West Scandinavian folklore. They were shape-shifters and often joined in human feasts and stole food. If you smelt cooking while out in the forest, you might be near a troll's dwelling.

All-seeing Herdsman
Argus

Many-eyed Argus burst into the satyr's hide-out. "You'll steal no more cattle from us!" he roared.

Tossing aside a bone, the satyr fired off arrow after arrow at the giant's heart. But Argus, tall as a tree, batted them off like pine needles blowing in the wind. As he smashed down his sword on the satyr's skull, the creature reeled back.

Argus whirled him around and flung him against a column. The satyr was now a bloody blotch on the stone. With a grunt of satisfaction, Argus turned and strode back to his herds of plump, glossy cattle.

How to defeat Argus

Because Argus had so many eyes, some were always open and watchful. Only the god Hermes was able to lull Argus with music and storytelling until all of his 100 eyes closed, and he struck the sleeping giant dead.

Where does this myth come from?

In Greek mythology, Argus was chosen by Hera, wife of Zeus, to guard a beautiful white heifer. This was really Io, a nymph with whom Zeus had fallen in love and turned into a heifer to protect her. After Argus was killed, Hera placed his eyes in the tail of her favourite bird, the peacock.

Beast Power

Strength
7

Repulsiveness
3

Special Powers
4

Ferocity
6

Invincibility
8

Total
28/50

One-eyed Colossus
Polyphemus

In their travels, the Greek hero Odysseus and his warriors landed on the island of Sicily. Here they ventured inside the hilltop cave of the one-eyed giant Polyphemus. All too soon the giant came thundering up the hill. Spying the tiny strangers, he boomed, "Hu –huuuumans!" Grabbing their weapons, the men scattered and tried to hide.

Two fled to the entrance but Polyphemus scooped one up, as if he were fishing a prawn out of a pool. The giant clamped his crooked teeth around his victim, while the other warrior froze in horror – he knew his turn was next.

How to defeat Polyphemus

Odysseus outwitted Polyphemus by getting him drunk, then blinding his one eye with a red-hot stake. He and his surviving men escaped, but to be completely safe it might be best to pierce an artery or vital organ while the giant was slumbering.

Where does this myth come from?

In Greek mythology, Polyphemus was the fiercest of the Cyclopes, a race of brutish, one-eyed giants. He was the son of the god Poseidon, ruler of the ocean, and has a cameo role in Homer's epic poem, the Odyssey. *This relates the adventures of Odysseus after the Trojan War. The blinding of Polyphemus enrages Poseidon, who makes Odysseus's journey long and hazardous.*

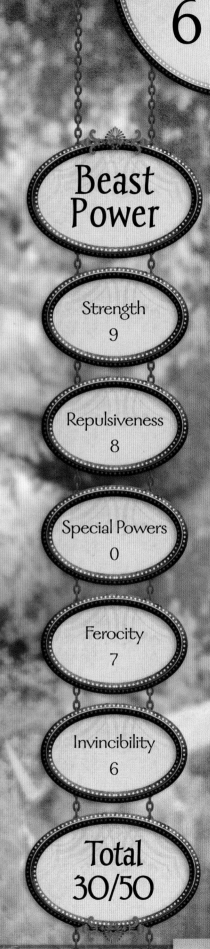

Beast Power

Strength
9

Repulsiveness
8

Special Powers
0

Ferocity
7

Invincibility
6

Total
30/50

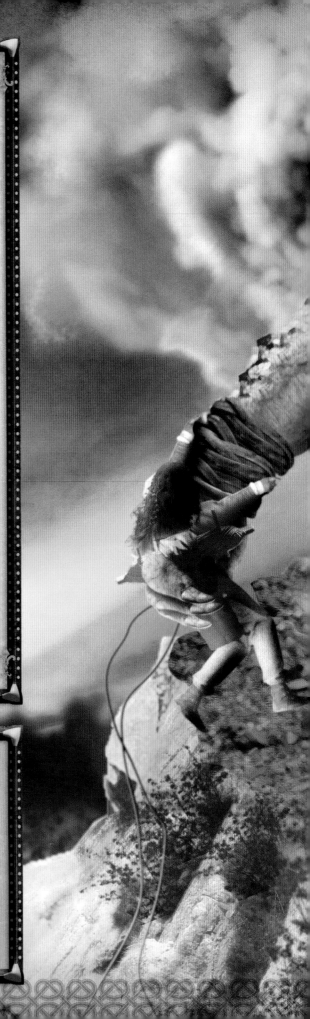

Mountain Savage
Mountain troll

The mountaineer hauled himself up to a high ledge that seemed nearer the sky than the valley below. At once he felt himself grabbed in a vice-like grip as an unearthly scream split his eardrums. "I shall eat your head before you have my treasure, vermin."

A massive, evil-looking troll was lifting him in the air. Its tiny, bloodshot eyes rolled in fury and it was draped in chains of gold.

"No one climbs my mountain and lives!" roared the troll. Wriggling, the man peered down towards the troll's feet, where he could see human bones scattered about. Aargh, was this to be his fate?

How to defeat a Mountain Troll

Since greedy trolls love gold, leave a trail of treasure outside its cave during a thunder storm — once hit by lightning, the troll will be well and truly frazzled.

Where does this myth come from?

Troll tales abound in Norse mythology (the ancient tales of Scandinavia) and in Norway especially are associated with the race of giants called Jötnar, who often warred with the gods. The word Trolleri means a kind of harmful magic, and trolls were thought to have the power to change themselves into storms, beasts or beautiful maidens.

Beast
Power

Strength
8

Repulsiveness
9

Special Powers
2

Ferocity
7

Invincibility
6

Total
32/50

Celtic Hero
Cuchulain

The battle fury was upon the mighty warrior Cuchulain. This fight with his opponent Ferdiad would decide an entire war. His muscles bulged and swelled, and his body seemed to grow to giant size. One eye stared madly, his hair stood on end, and his mouth stretched wide open, showing sharp, dog-like teeth flecked with fiery sparks.

"Cu-chu-lain! Cu-chu-lain!" chanted his fellow warriors. Leaping in the air, he grasped his deadly spear, the *gae bolga*, and aimed. With a horrible crunch, its barbed point hit Ferdiad's body just below his shield. He fell lifeless to the ground, blood spurting from the wound, as Cuchulain's men let out a deafening roar of triumph.

How to defeat *Cuchulain*

Dog meat is fatal to Cuchulain, and the only way is to trick him into eating it. This is exactly what happened when three witches in the guise of old women invited him to share their stew. He then lost his magical powers and was mortally wounded.

Where does this myth come from?

Cuchulain (pronounced Coo-shull-in) is a hero of Celtic folklore blessed with magical strength. His father was a god or warrior and his mother an Ulster princess. His exploits feature in ancient Irish tales about kings, queens, warriors, magicians, druids and sorceresses. Cuchulain's combat with Ferdiad decided the war between the armies of Ulster and Connaught.

Beast Power

Strength
8

Repulsiveness
7

Special Powers
4

Ferocity
8

Invincibility
8

Total
35/50

Cannibal Giants
Laestrygonians

Odysseus did not know that he had reached the island of a cannibal tribe called the Laestrygonians – until one of his scouts was grabbed and eaten by the king himself. The giants hurled boulders into the harbour, shattering Odysseus's ships like walnuts. Men dived overboard in terror, some hit by broken masts and splintered oars, mixing their blood with the foaming sea.

The Laestrygonians speared them like fish, carrying off the crew of 11 ships to make a fine and tasty banquet. Only Odysseus and his crew escaped with their lives.

How to defeat Laestrygonians
This would be a real challenge, and the only answer might be to give the giants a sleeping potion, then deliver a death blow.

Where does this myth come from?

These pitiless monsters of Greek mythology occur in Homer's Odyssey and cause the most disastrous episode of Odysseus's wanderings. The harbour where 11 of his ships are anchored is very narrow and sheltered, making them easy targets for the bloodthirsty giants. Odysseus has no choice but to row away with his crew as quickly as possible.

Beast Power

Strength
9

Repulsiveness
6

Special Powers
2

Ferocity
10

Invincibility
9

Total
36/50

Giant of Ice and Stone
Hrungnir

As Hrungnir and Thor faced each other, lightning split the sky and thunder boomed around the mountaintops. The god stood waist-high to Hrungnir, but his courage was legendary.

"Your puny sound effects don't frighten ME!" yelled Hrungnir. Thor laughed and whirled his magic hammer, Mjollnir, round his head, letting it fly at the very moment the giant hurled his whetstone.

The hammer crashed into the whetstone in mid-air, shattering it into razor-sharp arrowheads of flint. One hit Thor in the forehead and he staggered – but Mjollnir whirred onward, dead set on its course towards the huge stone head of Hrungnir…

How to defeat Hrungnir

Only a clever trick could vanquish Hrungnir. Perhaps he could be lured to a mountain top overlooking a lake to admire his stone face in the water. Then, if he leaned farther and farther over, he might topple right in.

Where does this myth come from?

One of the legends of Norse mythology, this episode was recounted in the 13th century in a famous work called the Prose Edda *by an Icelandic poet and chieftain, Snorri Sturluson. The mightiest giant of the icy Northern realms, Hrungnir once got drunk and declared he could kill all the gods of Asgard. So Thor challenged him to single combat…*

Beast Power

Strength
10

Repulsiveness
4

Special Powers
6

Ferocity
8

Invincibility
9

Total
37/50

King of all Trolls
King Troll

To the trolls it sounded like squeaking, but the man was really shrieking at the top of his voice as they dragged him before their king. He stopped yelling as his eyes took in the looming shape of King Troll. The legs were as thick as an old redwood, the hands ended in yellow claws, and below a mane of matted hair could be seen an ancient face seamed with furrows and a snarling mouth.

Licking his lips with a black tongue, King Troll grabbed the man and prepared to roast him on the fire. The other trolls squealed and capered about. How long before one more skull hung from the King's belt of trophies?

How to defeat King Troll

Salt is one way to get rid of trolls. It was thought to have magical powers that were stronger than those of the trolls. King Troll, though, would probably need a barrelful rather than a pinch!

Where does this myth come from?

A troll king, or 'Old Man of the Mountains', appears in a play called Peer Gynt *by the Norwegian dramatist Henrik Ibsen. The play was inspired by a Norwegian fairy tale featuring trolls, brownies, gnomes and witches. The king is called Dovregubben – he lives inside the Dovre Mountains with his court.*

Beast Power

Strength
9

Repulsiveness
9

Special Powers
3

Ferocity
8

Invincibility
9

Total
38/50

Rogues' Gallery

20 10

Cynocephalus

This dog-headed species was thought to live in India and North Africa. Some people think they were related to werewolves...

22 9

Geryon

The three-headed monster had a monster-hound called Orthrus. It had two heads and was the brother of Cerberus, guard dog of the Underworld.

30 6

Polyphemus

The Cyclops devoured four more of Odysseus's men before the others escaped. Enraged, he flung huge rocks at their boat as they rowed away.

32 5

Mountain Troll

Rich mountain trolls who hoarded treasure might take it out to air, and just to be doubly safe, set a bull or snake to guard it.

37 2

Hrungnir

The shattering of Hrungnir's whetstone was followed by the smashing of his head by Thor's hammer, Mjollnir. The giant crashed down on top of Thor, pinning the god to the ground. Thor was unable to move, even with the help of two other gods. Only his young son Magni was strong enough to lift up the dead giant and free him.

8

Forest Troll

Besides having twigs and branches instead of hair, this troll could morph into a log or tree stump. It could also make itself invisible.

26

7

Argus

The giant used his superhuman strength to kill a rampaging bull, and an even more destructive foe: the half-nymph, half-serpent, Echidna.

28

4

Cuchulain

The king gave Cuchulain his own weapons, since the warrior was so strong that all other swords and spears broke in his huge hands.

35

3

Laestrygonians

Odysseus's scouts first met the hideous queen of the Laestrygonians. She called for her husband, who tore one of the men in two and drank his blood.

36

1

King Troll

On one occasion, Thor himself was lured to the huge mountain castle of the Troll King Geirrodur. Here in the great hall, the Troll King snatched a piece of white-hot metal from the fire and flung it at Thor. The god caught it in his iron gloves and hurled it straight back. It burnt right through an iron pillar, the Troll King himself and the castle wall behind.

38

Want to Know More?

Trollery, Drollery

In Scandinavian folklore, the phrase 'being taken to the mountain' was code for being snatched by trolls. If the people ever came back, they might have lost their memory or their wits. Church bells rung long and loud could make trolls fall very ill, and a prisoner might escape their clutches that way. But a spiteful troll would always say, "Get out!" before trying finally to skewer the captive, so it would have been best to wait until he keeled right over.

Then there was the death-by-naming technique. A troll could not survive having his name shouted aloud, so never gave it away. The trick was to trick it out of him! A maiden captured by a troll called Dunker managed to do this, and when she named him, he exploded and the mountain around him collapsed, leaving her free to go home.

Norwegian trolls were the biggest of all, and had a variety of ugly features such as a big, flat or long, thin nose, crooked back, huge feet, over-long teeth, and leathery, scaly or hairy skin. Sometimes they had more than one head, or an extra eye in the middle of their forehead.

Many Scandinavian landmarks have the word 'troll' in them. For example, the *troldeskoven* or troll forests in Denmark are known for their ancient bent and twisted trees, the strange shapes being caused by wind and frost. Wander there at sunset and it could be you'll see a troll!

Boomerang Hammer

Thor and the other Norse gods possessed many magical weapons and accoutrements. His hammer, Mjollnir, was forged by two dwarf brothers. The trickster god Loki bet them his head that they could not make a hammer to outclass Odin's marvellous spear, Gungnir.

They accepted the bet but as they worked, Loki turned himself into a gadfly and stung one of the dwarfs to distract him. The handle ended up shorter than it should have been, so the hammer could only be wielded with one hand. But the gods voted it the most wonderful weapon of all – not only could it smash through mountains, but it always hit its target and returned to the hand of Thor.

And Loki? He wriggled out of losing his head by saying his neck was not part of the deal, and that they could not possibly avoid cutting off the tiniest part of his neck. Instead one of the dwarfs sewed his lips together to keep him quiet – for a change.

Labours of Hercules

Strong men often get tangled up with monsters as it is only they who have any chance of defeating them. One of the most famous is the Greek hero Hercules, who was given 12 almost-impossible tasks to perform by his master King Eurystheus. Hercules was actually the son of Zeus, so no wonder he had special powers.

Many of his labours involved killing or capturing animals – as with the cattle of Geryon. Probably the stinkiest was cleaning out the stables used by thousands of cattle belonging to King Augeas. They were piled high with dung which had not been cleared away for decades. The challenge was to clean up all this mess in a day. Hercules did so by diverting two nearby rivers to run through the stables and carry off the filth in one mighty, fast-running torrent. Since then the phrase 'cleaning out the Augean stables' has often been used to describe a horrible, grubby job of mountainous proportions.

Fighting for Ulster

Cuchulain had his very first adventure as a seven-year-old. King Conchobar of Ulster had a band of boy warriors and Cuchulain wanted to join them. To prove himself, he knocked them down one by one in single combat until they submitted to his leadership at last. One day, he came racing home from battle in his chariot, drawn by the twin horses that had been born on the same day as him.

He had hung the heads of three foes from the chariot, and was still frenzied with battle fury. To calm his rage, the king's warriors dipped him in three tubs of ice-cold water. The first one burst, the second boiled, but the third just got warm – so Cuchulain was perfectly cool again!

Index

A
Argus 14–15, 29

C
Celtic folklore 21
Cuchulain 20–21, 29, 31
Cyclopes 16–17, 28
Cynocephalus 8–9, 28

F
forest trolls 12–13, 29

G
Geryon 10–11, 28
Greek mythology 10, 15, 17, 23, 31

H
Hera 15
Hercules 10, 31
Hermes 15
Homer 17, 23
Hrungnir 24–25, 28

K
King Troll 26–27, 29

L
labours of Hercules 10, 31
Laestrygonians 22–23, 29
Loki 30

M
Mjollnir 25, 28, 30
mountain trolls 18–19, 28

N
Norse mythology 13, 19, 25, 30
Norwegian fairy tale 26

O
Odysseus 17, 22, 23
Odyssey 17, 23
Orthrus 28

P
Peer Gynt 26
Polo, Marco 8
Polyphemus 16–17, 28
Prose Edda 25

T
Thor 25, 28, 29, 30
trolls 30
    forest trolls 12–13, 29
    King Troll 26–27, 29
    mountain trolls 18–19, 28

The Author

Alice Peebles is an editor and writer specializing in the arts and humanities for children. She is a coauthor of Encyclopedia of Art for Young People and one of the creators of The Guzunder Gang audiobook series. She has also edited and written for several children's magazines focused on history, art, geography. She lives in London, England.

The Artist

Nigel Chilvers is a digital illustrator based in the United Kingdom. He has illustrated numerous children's books.